ECK WISDOM

on

Life After Death

ECK WISDOM

on
Life After Death

HAROLD KLEMP

ECKANKAR
Minneapolis
www.Eckankar.org

ECK Wisdom on Life after Death

Copyright © 2015, 2016 ECKANKAR

Printed in USA

Photo of Sri Harold Klemp (page 81) by Art Galbraith

Second edition—2016

Library of Congress Cataloging-in-Publication Data
Names: Klemp, Harold, author.
Title: ECK wisdom on life after death / Harold Klemp.
Other titles: Spiritual wisdom on life after death
Description: Second edition. | Minneapolis : Eckankar, 2016.
Identifiers: LCCN 2016043671 | ISBN 9781570434389 (pbk. : alk. paper)
Subjects: LCSH: Future life--Eckankar (Organization) | Eckankar (Organization)--Doctrines.
Classification: LCC BP605.E3 K574455 2016 | DDC 299/.93--dc23 LC record available at https://lccn.loc.gov/2016043671

♾ This paper meets the requirements of ANSI/NISO Z39.48-1992 (Permanence of Paper).

Contents

A Visit to Heaven

$\mathcal{L}$enny was a seeker.

Years ago, Lenny had gone hunting in a neighbor's field with his father, brother, and a neighbor friend. Tragedy was to change Lenny's life. Lightning struck both him and his neighbor, who died immediately. Lenny himself went into cardiac arrest. His brother revived him en route to the hospital. In the emergency room, however, Lenny's heart then failed again.

The medical staff tried everything in its power to revive him, but without success. Grave, hopeless seconds flew away like falcons upon the wind. Unable to make out a sign of life, the doctor signaled a nurse to pull the plug. As she bent over to disconnect the

1

monitors, the faintest bleep sounded from the EKG.

Life!

The team sprang into action, reviving Lenny.

He lay in a coma for six hours. But seemingly unconscious, he'd actually awakened out of the body, in the inner worlds.

A realm of stunning beauty greeted him. There he found delightful rest and peace. His was a flood of bliss and ecstasy. And in that place of unspeakable love, Lenny caught sight of his neighbor, who'd been struck by lightning and translated (died). The man was lingering near a stairway leading to an even greater light. He motioned Lenny to join him; they'd ascend the stairs together. But Lenny shook his head. No, there was still plenty to see and do on earth.

Then a man with a snowy beard and in a long white robe addressed him. Was this God? (Lenny was to learn later that this exalted being would never, ever make a pretense of being God.) The old man spoke of the changes to come for Lenny: his future.

Lenny met other beings too. One especially striking man had a gleaming bald head, but more about that later.

Lenny could recall only fragments of his inner conversations with those beings, though the beauty and tranquillity of that world were like an exquisite script engraved upon his heart. His remembrance of that celestial place enfolded him in an aura of peace and contentment. So profound and pure, in fact, was this recollection that he would spend many fruitless years trying either to recapture or escape its memory.

Lenny regained consciousness. Later Lenny's doctor would confide to him what a miracle his recovery had been. Such things did not happen; it was simply unheard of. The doctor, badly shaken by Lenny's amazing recovery, could not understand how he ever survived. It defied all reason.

For the next twenty years Lenny tried to blot his near-death experience from memory. He desperately wanted to get on with living, yet the exquisite splendor of that divine love continued to haunt him. So Lenny felt like a misfit in society.

Ten years after leaving the hospital, tragedy struck again.

Lenny's best friend suffered a massive heart attack and died in his arms. The shock of it brought to mind memories of his own near-death experience. No question about it, his friend was rejoicing in the very love and peace that Lenny had once enjoyed too. Every waking hour since his best friend's death, Lenny tried to recapture that elusive feeling of total love and acceptance.

A few years ago, Lenny's own life began to unravel. For one thing, his marriage crumbled. Then, his career went up in smoke. He'd lost everything worth living for. Gone. Everything was gone. Yet even during this storm of pain and turmoil, Lenny could feel a guiding hand directing his affairs.

Who or what was this silent presence?

One day, seized by despair while out driving, Lenny cried, "What's going on? Help me! I give up! Do with me what you will. I need help!"

At that very moment, a white car swerved in front of him. Its bumper sticker read "ECKANKAR 1-800-LOVE GOD." *Curious*, he thought.

Soon he began to notice those bumper stickers everywhere.

Tossing and turning one night, Lenny realized he was spiritually on the edge of a precipitous cliff. He crawled from under his covers and switched on the TV. On the screen was an ad for the ECK Worldwide Seminar in Minneapolis, Minnesota. A voice inside him said, "Call the number."

Lenny hesitated. "Call the number!" So he dialed 1-800-LOVE GOD.

A short while later, a mailing arrived from Eckankar. Inside it was a free book, *ECKANKAR—Ancient Wisdom for Today*. He skimmed it; he liked it. All right, then, it was time to visit the Temple of ECK in Chanhassen, Minnesota.

Lenny, a Minnesota resident, had driven past the temple for ten years. He'd always known he'd stop in someday, but a certain timidity kept him from it.

He finally overcame his reluctance and went to the temple. Inside, a genial host offered him a tour, to which Lenny agreed. The tour coursed along a corridor to a chapel near the main sanctuary. There, on a wall, hung color portraits of ECK Masters.

Lenny stared at them. For the first time since his near-death experience, he finally understood his out-of-the-body journey. He recognized the ECK Master Fubbi Quantz.

He was the man with the white beard and long white robe. He was the very one Lenny had once mistaken for God, the one who'd told him things about his future.

And there, too, was a portrait of Yaubl Sacabi, the bald-headed man who'd offered guidance in times of trouble.

For the first time in twenty years, Lenny knew with absolute certainty that his experience had been real. He wasn't crazy; in fact, he was blessed.

In good time, Lenny learned about karma, reincarnation, and past lives, and he also found answers to a lifetime of questions. Best of all, he discovered the way to again enter those worlds of light, love, and infinite beauty he'd seen so many years ago. It is through the Spiritual Exercises of ECK.

Divine Evolution

*Y*ou are Soul—an eternal, individual spark of God, who can never die. Each person is a divine being who comes to life on earth with a spiritual purpose. Lifetime after lifetime, Soul grows in love and grace, ultimately to become a Co-worker with God.

A lifetime is a precious gift, an opportunity for spiritual growth and service to others. Most of all, life brings Soul the purity of love, compassion, and grace.

Death is a doorway, a transition into the inner worlds. Births and deaths mark the journey of Soul. The translation, or movement, from one stage of experience to another is but a further step on Soul's journey home to God.

The great fear behind all fears is the fear of death. Death is such an absolute term. It means that's the end of everything. That's how people think of death. But if we look at the spiritual matter of the death of the physical body, we in Eckankar prefer the term *translation*; we say someone has *translated*.

Think of it in terms of translating one language to another—like from English into German, or from German into English or French. The meaning and content, the essence, is the same. Likewise, Soul is the same and can carry Its body of knowledge from one lifetime into another.

The purpose of the ECK teachings is to make you aware of yourself as Soul. You begin to realize your ability to move beyond the physical body even while you are still alive in the body. When Saint Paul said, "I die daily," he referred to this process. It is similar to death in that in the Soul body, one actually leaves the physical body to take a look at the worlds beyond.

Here one gains confidence and courage and becomes acquainted with the other worlds, so that when the time comes, Soul moves through the transition very smoothly, very naturally. Death loses its sting; the grave loses its victory.

Sometimes the transition is made so gradually that the person who is near death finds it a pleasant experience. I remember the way my grandmother would sit by her sewing machine and seem to be talking to herself. But she wasn't at all. She was speaking with friends and relatives from the other side; she was already able to see them.

This often happens with people who are about to die. The transition is very gradual, and you know they are in good hands. The person who leaves this plane generally does not miss it. There's no reason to, once you realize the continuity of life.

When we leave the physical body permanently—if we are advanced to any degree at all—there need be no concern for this life on earth, for we have moved into a far greater expression of it. Our divine evolution is a wonderful thing.

In most cases, as we make the transition into the heavenly worlds, we are totally unconcerned about it. As bright as the sunlight appears to our eyes, this physical world is a dark, small, mean place compared to the other worlds. You will see settings similar to those on earth, but larger and with a lot more light.

There will be a lightness and spaciousness about the body that you wear there. Soul is once again wearing a body, but It is on a higher plane. It is so natural that generally you don't give it a second thought. And you are always greeted by someone you know and love.

For people who love truth and love God, it's a smooth change. The key really is love.

THE ETERNAL NATURE OF SOUL

𝒯here once was a handsome Trojan named Tithonus. Lucky was he to have the love of Eos, goddess of the dawn.

Tithonus prayed to Eos to grant him immortality. But he'd neglected to ask for youth. So in time, like any mortal, Tithonus became aged in body and infirm.

He now offered up a new prayer. Would Eos let him die?

This boon she could not grant, but she could change him into a new physical form, and so, Tithonus became a grasshopper.

Of course, each Soul is eternal—like Tithonus. Unlike him, however, the True

Self has no fear of the hand of aging, infirmity, or forgetfulness. It is whole, beyond time. Yet the human bodies It wears during Its many rebirths do see the afflictions that come with the passing of years.

A human shell is like an oak leaf. It buds in spring, enjoys its beauty, vibrancy, and strength in summer, then turns dry after the chill winds of autumn. In winter, it falls.

But then, spring.

A new bud shoots forth, and a new cycle of life begins.

Soul takes on a new body in like manner. In our human incarnations we are like an oak leaf: each time a leaf, but not the same leaf. In fact, Soul, the immortal, is rather like Tithonus the grasshopper. On each return, we hop from one set of circumstances to a somewhat different set.

And yet, the grasshopper's memory is short. He's aware of one jump at a time.

But barely that.

So where does this leave people who return to earth again and again in a new body? They are like Tithonus. The round of births and rebirths will carry them tumultuously through the ages. They will hop from life to life, wondering what it's all about.

A truth seeker learns it's about spiritual liberation. It's about finding a way out.

It's about freedom, joy, and wisdom. It's all about divine love.

Someday, each grasshopper will catch the high wind of ECK and fly to a place of incredible light and beauty.

God's full love awaits them.

WHY REINCARNATION?

$\mathcal{L}$inda's friend, Georgie, died suddenly in a car accident. This was a real shock to her, because she'd never lost anyone close to her before. To her, death meant the end of existence. And the idea that Georgie no longer existed was something Linda couldn't quite deal with. She fell into a deep despondency, crying a lot, trying to figure out what had happened to Georgie.

Then one night as she was lying in bed, she saw Georgie standing by her bed.

"Georgie, how are you doing?" Linda said.

"Fine," Georgie answered.

"But you're dead; you don't exist," she said.

15

"Well, as you can see, I'm here."

Linda looked at Georgie in awe. *He must know what it's like on the other side*, she realized. "I've always felt that death meant the end of existence," she told him. "But you are here."

"Yeah, if you want to see, come along. I'll show you," Georgie said.

"No, I've got to take care of my baby," Linda remembered. "I can't leave now."

"Don't worry," he said, "I can bring you back." And since Linda trusted her friend, she said, "OK."

Georgie took her into the Causal Plane, into an area where the Akashic records are stored, the seed place of all the karma of past lives. She saw these long chutes or slides, like farmers use in barn lofts for dropping hay to the cattle below. Souls, looking like adult human beings, were standing at the top of the slide. As they slid down, they kept changing form until they became infants. Then they'd plop down into the world, crying and wondering what had happened. It was a cold, dark world after the light of the Causal Plane.

The Slide of Reincarnation

These Souls had been adults who had died on earth and gone to the Causal Plane to await their time of reincarnation. They'd get on this slide of reincarnation and go sliding right back into another body on earth. But the babies only had a small memory in the back of their minds of who and what they'd been in their previous lives.

Linda realized that the death of the physical body here on earth is not the death of the personality. The personality lives beyond the death of the human body.

We're not talking about Soul now, we're talking about the personality: the Astral, Causal, and Mental bodies of the individual. Not until Soul is reincarnated does the personality die. This is why so many times after a parent or a loved one dies, people have dream experiences with that person.

Why? They are seeing these people as the personality, or the complex that the personality stands for, meaning the Astral or Causal body.

When the physical body dies, the person takes up residence on the Astral Plane. It's pretty much the same as here on earth, except the person may take on a younger appearance. But the personality itself is extinguished when that individual goes down the slide of reincarnation and comes back to earth.

This explains why you see your loved ones or even pets in your dreams after they have passed on.

Reincarnation Clears Up Mysteries

Many people don't understand there is a reason for inequalities. Why some people are born as geniuses and others as slow learners.

Some have been here many lifetimes. Musicians, for example, may have practiced for lifetimes before this one. They pick up their interest in music when they come back. People call them geniuses, and they think it's a big mystery how Mozart could possibly play the piano at age four.

Reincarnation clears up a lot of mysteries. This is part of what Eckankar has to offer you. Yet beyond reincarnation and karma (cause and effect), which are part of our teachings, there is something more.

This something more is divine love.

Soul Exists Because God Loves It

There's no way to miss out on the blessings of God unless you turn your back on the love and thanks that are yours as a gift. Linda had learned the love and thanks that come from trust in someone she had known as a friend.

Georgie was the kind of person she thought she'd like to marry someday. But

Georgie never noticed her in that way; she was just a friend of his sister's. So Linda never got to marry Georgie, and then suddenly Georgie was gone. That left her in a deep state of grief and despondency. But through this bond of divine love, Georgie came back. He came back to show Linda that there is more to life than she had ever known before.

Georgie existed because he was Soul, and Soul exists because God loves It. That is why there is no such thing as eternal death. The teachings of Eckankar give hope to people who have no hope.

How do you get off the wheel of karma?

You're going to have to go through your lessons until the experiences of life give you the wisdom, love, and understanding that you need to someday take a step higher on the spiritual ladder and ultimately become a Co-worker with God.

This is the goal in ECK: to become a Co-worker with God.

Do Animals Go to Heaven?

$\mathcal{W}$ill Rogers, a comedian in the mid-1930s, during the Great Depression, once said, "If there are no animals in heaven, I want to go to the place where the animals are."

That was his opinion, and it's interesting that he was so far ahead of his time. Because today people are wondering, Are cats and dogs and goldfish and all kinds of pretty little birds all going to be in heaven too?

The standard version of heaven is that all these things won't be there. Well, in the ECK heaven, these things are there too, so don't worry.

Heaven is inside us. None can point to

a place and say, "It's here" or "It's there." It is a state of consciousness. As Soul moves to higher states of consciousness, It may choose to live and serve in places of more love and beauty. So people think that heaven is a place.

Higher Souls may live in finer places.

Yet heaven is not a place. It is a state of consciousness.

Zeke's Translation

A man had a very old dog, Zeke, who was his special friend. The veterinarian had bad news, though. The fourteen-and-a-half-year-old dog had cancer in his abdomen, but no pain.

He'd probably slip peacefully away, said the vet. But if Zeke developed a breathing problem, it would be time to let him go.

That sad day soon came. The man and his wife took Zeke to the vet and had him put to sleep. Zeke was in the man's arms when he went, literally leaping from that tired old body like a prisoner set free from his cell.

On the drive home, the man's Spiritual Eye opened. He saw Prajapati, the ECK Master who cares for the animals.

Prajapati was standing on a hill near a tree. Behind him came a stream of bright golden sunlight from the sky. But there was also a ball of light, and the man knew instinctively that it was his departed friend, Zeke, in the Soul body.

Zeke's joy was unbounded.

By telepathic voice, Zeke said to the man, "Daddy, I'm free! Thank you for all the love."

Many people love their pets very much and feel a deep sense of loss when they pass over. And they often worry, Is that the end? Does my dear friend simply cease to be?

Soul is eternal. Soul lives on in the next world, just as It did in this one.

And, if it is right for that Soul, It can come back to earth in another body, sometimes to the same family It was with before.

Is God's love even sufficient for animals? Yes, it very clearly is. At least it is clear to those who have the eyes to see and the spiritual awareness to recognize this eternal truth.

Kitten Dreams

A woman we'll call Katie had a female cat for a pet. They had lived together for eleven years, and there was a very strong bond of love between them. Eventually the cat died, and Katie missed her very much.

About a year after her cat had died, Katie had a series of very clear dreams. In one dream, someone told her, "Your cat is going to reincarnate on Monday, July 31."

When Katie woke up, she said to herself, *That dream was very nice. But I live in an apartment in a big city now. I don't know how my cat is going to find me.*

Then she had a second dream. In this dream someone handed her two tiny kittens.

Both kittens were striped; one was lighter, the other darker. The Inner Master told her, "The darker of the striped kittens is yours."

That week one of Katie's friends called. "Two of my cats had litters at the same time," she said. "Would you like a kitten?"

When Katie went to look at one of the litters, she immediately saw the striped kittens from her dream. "This is my cat," she said, picking up the darker of the striped kittens.

"It's a male," said her friend.

Katie paused. "A male?" she said. "My cat was a very feminine female. I can't imagine her coming back as a male cat." Suddenly she was unsure of her dream.

Her friend said, "If you want a female, there's a lovely gray-and-white kitten in the other litter. This kitten loves everybody." But the kitten didn't love Katie.

"All right," sighed Katie, putting down the clawing animal. "I think I'd better stick with the first striped kitten."

On her way out she asked her friend, "By the way, what was the mother cat's name?" "Z," said the cat owner. Z is another name for the Inner Master, Wah Z.

As she drove home, Katie said inwardly, "Maybe this really is my cat, even though it's a male."

Later, before her daily contemplation, she picked up *The Shariyat-Ki-Sugmad*, the Eckankar bible. She opened the book at random and read, "Soul will alternate between male and female bodies, each time learning some lessons and gathering karma and working off karma."

Katie received the answer she needed.

Animals are often examples to people of how the spiritual laws work.

LOVE NEVER DIES

*A*n article in *Psychology Today* reported a study that said the death of a loved one is among the things most feared. But whether it's the loss of a loved one, a serious illness, or financial worries, the lesson is that love binds all wounds. If troubles do not bring one the capacity for love, then his whole life will have been in vain.

Love is the only thing that can replace a loss of the heart, and Soul Travel (which is an expansion of spiritual awareness) is the gateway to love. Soul, as long as It is under the temporal conditions of the lower planes, will have losses of many kinds. But Soul, knowing of Its divine nature, sees beyond the ends of eternity and knows It can never be extinguished like a candle's flame.

The Narrow Doorway

My eye doctor had lost his father earlier this year. In the final weeks of his father's last illness, the doctor had dropped everything on weekends to fly from Minneapolis to Arizona to visit him.

Unexpectedly, he said, "The door to heaven must be narrow."

A twinkle in his eye begged the question, Why?

The doctor and his father had grown very close over the past few years, so death had left a big vacuum in the doctor's life.

"My dad was nearly ninety," he said, "and had been a rather stocky man most of his life. But he was very thin when he finally left.

"The same with others I've known," he went on. "So the door to heaven must be very narrow."

We had a laugh about that.

On a more serious note, he recounted the last days of his father. The old man had lived a long, full life, yet he clung eagerly to this life, uncertain about what the next had to offer. But as time passed, he began to have inner experiences of a bright white place. Ahead of him in the vision stood a white staircase. It led up to a door.

Yet no matter how hard he tried to get through the door to a new life in the heavenly worlds, he couldn't get it open. It frustrated him to no end.

Then he'd open his eyes in the hospital room, look at his son, and say, "I'm not in heaven yet, am I?"

"How do you know that?" his son asked.

"Because you're still sitting here."

They enjoyed a good laugh.

Then, his father had gone on, happy and content at his good fortune in having mastered the secret to opening the door at

29

the top of the white staircase. However, he left behind a very reflective and lonesome son, the doctor.

"The passing of one's parents can be a traumatic event," I said, addressing his unspoken fear. "It means we're next in line."

He smiled ruefully, relieved that someone had put a handle on the cup for him.

When the eye exam was over, I made as if to get up from the chair, because my wife, Joan, wanted him to recheck her prescription. The conversation and exam had eaten into his lunch hour, but he seemed grateful for two sympathetic listeners. So he waved his hand for me to stay seated a moment more.

"Since you're here," he said, "may I ask you a question? What do you know about parallel worlds?"

The doctor is a Christian; his father was a benevolent agnostic who simply didn't know what to think about the hereafter. He was perfectly satisfied to enjoy the fruits of this life: his wife, family, friends, good health, and profession. His heaven was earth. That's all he could be certain of, and it pleased him.

Our good friend the doctor now felt a desire to know where his father was and how he was doing. Hence, the question about parallel worlds.

"Going into the heavenly worlds while still in the human body is the key to Soul Travel and dream travel," Joan and I said between us. He looked uncertain of how to use either to accomplish his desire of meeting his dad again.

"Love is stronger than fear or even death," I said. "Whenever there is a strong bond of love between two people, they can meet again in their dreams or by Soul Travel."

But the doctor, the Christian, hesitated.

I continued: "A master you trust spiri-

31

tually, like Christ, can make it happen. Just ask him in your prayers. He can take you to your father in a dream. He'll take care of all the details so you won't have to learn the dream methods yourself."

That agreed with him. An air of tranquillity now settled upon his face. He thought for a moment longer, then smiled.

Heaven's narrow door?

Yes, an individual must indeed leave behind all attachment to the things of this world before it's possible to go through heaven's door.

Abandon all things but one.

Pure love.

It is the key that opens the door to the highest place in heaven—God's home of Love and Mercy.

Spiritual Guidance during Times of Grief

*S*urely, the most difficult times we face occur at the translation, or parting, of loved ones. Yet life prepares us all along with temporary separations by distance and, yes, even of heart.

These temporary separations are many: a child goes to school the first time while the parents put on a brave face and offer hugs, kisses, and words of encouragement. A family's youth goes away to college. More distressful, perhaps, a youth goes into the military during times of war.

Life deals us thousands of such cards, each of which delivers a separation of heart or distance. And the pain that comes of it. They temper us. They teach us about the transitory nature of everything around us in this on-again, off-again world. And yet, all those occasions of temporary separation may instead have led us to a resistance to change.

Nevertheless, ready or not, life deals out cards of what seem like absolute separations of forever.

Our loved ones die and leave us in mourning.

These occasion the most difficult periods of all. A child loses a beloved grandparent and falls into a state of depression. Or, a child's pet translates. Where did whatever gave it warmth and movement go? A parent tries to explain.

Explanations to the bereaved about the nature of death heal nothing of consequence. The mind may accept the salve, but the heart cannot. Words alone will not heal a broken heart.

Only love—and time—can make things right.

What is the most beneficial service to a friend who grieves a translated mate? Is it advice? Perhaps a recitation of our own losses and a recital of dark nights again turned into bright days? No, only the most calloused of friends would thus cause more pain.

Silence (a listening ear) and service will find the most appreciation. And expression of love too.

We express our love and support in simple words and in necessary chores. We help make funeral arrangements if needed, shovel walks, or mow the lawn. We call friends or business associates of the departed to ease the burden of details from a sorrowful Soul.

We make ourself a magnet for love. We do so by letting love enter our heart, without compromise or hindrance.

Let divine love illuminate you, spiritualize your heart. Especially in the hours surrounding a loved one's loss of a dear one, lift your state of consciousness.

Near-Death Experience Brings Spiritual Help

When Marion, a girl from Germany, was fourteen years old, she got meningitis. A bacterial infection turned serious, and in just a matter of hours she went into a coma.

Her parents called an ambulance; Marion was rushed off to a hospital.

While the ambulance was driving along, Marion found herself out of the body for the first time. She was standing next to the stretcher in the ambulance. The paramedics couldn't stand up straight in the ambulance, but she could, because she was a viewpoint, in the Soul body.

Marion said, "Hey, this is pretty good. I'm there, but I'm here too." She realized that life didn't have to be just in that body, but life was here too.

When they got to the hospital, the doctors hooked Marion up to life support. She was mostly out of the body all this time, but one time she came back in. Just as she did, the heart monitor started going crazy, a long steady screech. That meant her heart had stopped. She was back in the other worlds again.

This time Marion saw a brilliant blue light, all around her. And with it came a humming sound.

The humming sounded like a high-powered generator. It's one of the sounds that an individual can hear in the other planes, one of the Sounds of God. It came with the Blue Light, which often refers to the Mahanta, the Living ECK Master, the spiritual leader of Eckankar.

The Seeker and the Master

This Blue Light is part of the Master's ability, part of his duties, to act as the Outer and the Inner Master of the seeker.

The Master of Eckankar is only the Master of ECKists. He isn't the master of the whole world; he isn't the master of Christians or Muslims or Jews—just ECKists. And all those who have been in Eckankar before.

Marion saw this Blue Light and heard this humming sound. She looked at the doctors working frantically over her, trying to bring life back to her body. But Marion realized, "Hey, I'm Soul. That's my body."

Sometimes it takes spiritual experience to get it right, to get the horse before the cart again. She said, "I'm Soul. I live. I don't need that body to live. Everything's beautiful and happy."

Traveling Out of the Body

Marion rose up in the air, looking from high above at the hospital. As she went up further, she found herself in a broad, green meadow.

It's a little bit like on *Star Trek*. The crew is on the starship *Enterprise*, and a couple of them get into the transporter. They stand very still, their atoms break down, and they're transported to a planet or another spaceship. They dematerialize here and re-form there.

This is what happens on the inner planes when Soul moves. This is the quick way. There are also some preliminary stages, where there is a sense of movement, sometimes a rushing or a roaring sound like a jet. But other times it's simply like dematerializing here and reforming there. Suddenly you're there.

Time and space are collapsed. You don't have to go through the laborious, time-consuming process of going through space. To go from one point in space to another usually takes time, but you can do away with all that.

Meeting Gopal Das

Marion found herself standing on a huge, beautiful lawn. There was dew on the grass, she was barefoot, and she had on some sort of light clothing. In the distance, coming down from the green hill, she saw a figure.

As the figure came closer, she saw it was a tall man in a white robe. As he got even closer she saw he had long blond hair to his shoulders and bright blue eyes. He came up to her, and she could see that his aura was full of harmony and energy. This aura engulfed her.

The man took her hand. "Welcome," he said. "Let me show you the Kingdom of God, and then you can return to the physical plane with refreshed memory and knowledge, and wait until the time is ready for you to begin your mission."

Marion didn't know this was the ECK Master Gopal Das.

Some people mistake him for Jesus Christ. But often it's Gopal Das, even though Jesus Christ does work on the inner planes and some of you have met him. Each of these masters has a place and works in the far worlds.

You might say, "No such thing can be possible. Heaven is this huge room with God the Father sitting there, and on his right hand or somewhere nearby is his son." And how big is he? "I'm not sure," you might say. What does he look like? "He has blond hair, white robe," you say. And what do people do in eternity?

But these are issues that really have nothing to do with the spiritual advancement of anyone. That is a state of being that is whatever it is. There are steps to it; there are different degrees of consciousness, even as there are manifestations of the places where people express these states of consciousness. These different places are the different levels of heaven.

After Gopal Das gave Marion this greeting, she went back into the body. It took her a number of weeks to recover enough to leave the hospital. But after this out-of-body experience and meeting Gopal Das, she remembered. She remembered other experiences she had with him. And she started looking for him.

Marion had to look for eighteen years before she made her first contact with Eckankar.

She always thought of Gopal Das as her guardian angel—this blond-headed, tall man, very fair of face, with a good feeling about him because he had this good aura.

Years later she met an ECKist who in time became her husband. And after a while, she told him this story.

"Here are some pictures of ECK Masters. Maybe he's one of them," her husband said. (There are a lot of other ECK Masters besides the handful shown in ECK pictures.)

Marion recognized the picture of Gopal Das. "That's him," she said.

She came into ECK because of this near-death experience, her first out-of-body experience when she met an ECK Master.

Why was it Gopal Das who met her, and not someone else? Sometimes the Mahanta, the Living ECK Master will send a certain ECK Master to a certain individual because they had a past-life connection. Marion had been a spiritual student of Gopal Das in some past lifetime. They had a bond of love between them, a spiritual bond. This is what she knew and understood, and so he came.

Gopal Das was the Mahanta, the Living ECK Master in Egypt, about 3000 BC. He now teaches the ECK bible, the Shariyat-Ki-Sugmad, which means Way of the Eternal. He teaches it on the Astral Plane, in the Temple of Golden Wisdom there.

The Mahanta as Inner Guide and Protector

In Eckankar, an earnest seeker is under the protection of a spiritual guide known as the Mahanta, the Living ECK Master. This is the Spiritual Traveler. As the Mahanta he is the Inner Master, the one who comes on the other planes to impart knowledge, truth, and wisdom.

The Mahanta is a state of consciousness. It is a spiritual state of consciousness very much like the Buddha consciousness or the Christ consciousness. The other half of the Spiritual Traveler's title is the Living ECK Master. This means the outer spiritual teacher, myself.

The teachings of Eckankar speak very directly and very distinctly of the two parts of the Master: the Inner Master and the Outer Master. The Inner Master is the Mahanta, and the Outer Master is the Living ECK Master.

The Inner Master is not a physical being. It is someone you see in the inner planes during contemplation or in the dream state. He may look like me, he may look like another ECK Master, or he may even look the same as Christ. All it is, really, is the merging of the Light and Sound of God into a matrix, into a form which appears as a person. This, then, becomes the inner guide which steers a person through the pitfalls of karma, the troubles we make for ourselves through ignorance of the spiritual laws.

The Mahanta is Lord of all worlds and escorts his disciple on the journey through the frontiers of death. The journey is a joyful one, for the Mahanta comes to the initiate in the last moments and says, "Are you ready, my beloved?" There is no hesitation, for the individual is delighted to see his old friend and is helped out of the rumpled clothing of his physical body. The Sound and Light of the Mahanta surround him, and they begin a leisurely passage through pastures of flowers and along serene riverbanks.

Therefore, the chela (spiritual student) is never alone for a moment but is greeted immediately by the Mahanta at the time of translation. There is no waiting in the courtyard of the King of the Dead, for the all-powerful Master is by his side. Do not grieve for those who die in ECK, for they are the most fortunate of all.

An ECK initiate tells of her encounter with death. She got the flu, and her fever climbed to a serious level. Suddenly, the Angel of Death appeared at her bedside, but, just as quickly, the Mahanta was there and said, "She is my chela; you have no power over her." Then to her, he said, "Come, it's time to go," and they stepped into the white Light.

This experience was to answer two questions for her: (1) Does Soul retain any connection with the body after death, and (2)

Is there any pain during cremation?

As she stood beside the Mahanta, he showed her how Soul left the body as white light. Indeed, a complete separation of Soul from the physical body took place. How could there be pain in cremation without a connection between body and Soul? She realized that only through Soul can the physical and all other bodies experience life here in the lower worlds. She was not separated from herself but was fully conscious as she stood beside the Master. The plight of the physical body did not concern her in the least.

Then she saw her husband's vigil by her sickbed. She felt such great love for him and could sense his loneliness and despair. Her light wrapped around him to ease his pain. The Mahanta saw this great love she had for her husband and said to her, "You can stay because you already have a heart of gold." But she hesitated and said, "Beloved Mahanta, while I love my husband beyond anything that I know, you come always first. And if you say I must go with you, I will."

The Master then said to her, "Love is the greatest power there is. Because you love so much, I will let you return to the physical body. You will, of course, have great pain with this sickness—a pain that need not be but is your choice." The Mahanta gives choices which the Angel of Death cannot give.

Before returning her to the physical body, the Mahanta took her into the inner planes and showed her such secrets as the source of all creations in the lower planes. They stood in the Blue Light, and he said, "This is where all creations start. We are at the beginning of life." Before she reentered her fevered body, he said, "You are being returned and, in exchange, must give total service to the ECK, the Holy Spirit." When she got into the body, she was very sick but soon recovered.

A humorous sidelight is that the next night the Angel of Death came again and stood by her bed. He said, "I'd love to take you, but I have no power over you." The dark angel had just come to have a last look.

Grief is for those who stay behind. The Soul that is freed of the body delights in the Sound and Light, and in the fullness of being.

QUESTIONS AND ANSWERS

*A*s spiritual leader of Eckankar, I get thousands of letters from seekers of truth around the world. All want direct and useful answers about how to travel the road to God. Here are several questions I've been asked about life after death.

Read on for clues that might help you.

When a Loved One Dies

My husband died suddenly while I was away at work. It was a great shock to me, and I feel terrible that I was not there when he went. Can you help me understand why this happened?

Your husband had finished learning what he had set out to learn in this lifetime. All the struggles within him to understand how he stood with God are resolved. It's his choice whether to serve God on the higher planes or to return to earth at a later time. For the time being he is quite satisfied on the Soul Plane, for there are many regions left to explore there.

It will be possible to meet with him via the dream state or Soul Travel if you have a strong desire to do so.

Please do not feel guilty that you were not at home during his translation from this physical life. It was the way he wanted it, to spare you from things he knew at the end, but which would not have been possible to explain to another. He is happy.

You will miss him, of course, because the absence of loved ones in the physical leaves one empty at first. But in six months you will look back at yourself and be surprised at how well you have adjusted to this very great change in your life.

Human Love and Love for God

Our five-year-old daughter passed on un-expectedly. She lit up my life to a degree I can-not describe. My son says she came to teach us about love. I would like to believe that my love for her is the love of God. Please help us during these difficult times.

The hand of sorrow has touched your family deeply. The wisdom of your son is right: Your daughter came to teach you all to love each other more.

We understand that life is a series of comings and goings, but somehow the pass-ing of a child is harder to accept than is the passing of one well along in years. It is hard to see now, but life will replace the joy you have lost with even greater joy. But first you must heal your sorrow, and that will take time.

Any words I write to you about the loss of your daughter cannot heal the ache of your heart. I would suggest that in contemplation you ask to meet the Mahanta as a family, including your daughter, of course. You will receive the understanding you need about human love being the link to love for God and the Mahanta.

Soul Is Eternal

Eleven years ago, our son committed suicide. This year our neighbor's boy did the same. What happens to those who do this? I just don't understand why he wanted to leave so badly.

We can only do so much when our dear ones shut out love and destroy themselves. Yet, take comfort: Soul is eternal.

You did all that was humanly possible to encourage him to anchor himself in this life. Please do not feel that you have failed him in any way. He knows you haven't and does not want you to carry an unnecessary burden of grief over time.

For a while, these unfortunate Souls wander in one of the inner worlds, the Astral

Plane, lost. Some must relive their act of self-harm again and again.

Thereby they learn how precious life is.

Eventually, the wheel of karma turns, and they are reborn. Their new life may be harsh, but it is to teach them love.

Your son's act of self-harm is of a temporary nature, for finally he, as Soul, will recognize his responsibility to life and serve it gladly without regrets. The Mahanta is working with him even now to help him adjust his spiritual viewpoint, so that he may become worthy of service to God.

Helping Others with Their Grief

How can I help a friend from another religion whose child recently died?

It would help first to understand the consciousness of many people in society as they face death with their families and loved ones. They are trying to come to grips with their beliefs about God.

Often they have been taught that God gives only good, but now all of a sudden here comes something bad. And how do you pray to God to take away the pain, they wonder, when maybe God gave them the pain? These are questions in the hearts of people like your friend.

At times, we try to give comfort to others but say just the wrong thing: "Your child is now in heaven, and he is much happier there" or "God gave you this cross to bear because you were strong enough to bear it." "Oh, that I had been weaker," the friend cries.

Nothing can heal your friend's grief but time. Man grapples with the meaning of life, and eventually he comes to certain terms with it.

Dealing with the Pain of Separation

It's been five months since my son was killed in an airplane accident. Although I have accepted his going and see him in my dreams often, I miss his physical presence. Tell me, how do I grieve?

The pain of losing a loved one is a sorrow common to all people, regardless of belief. It's natural to miss someone who has been so much a part of ourselves.

How does a person grieve? There's no one way because our feelings about each loved one who leaves are different in each case.

To deal with the pain of separation, make an effort to help others. Offer to babysit someone else's children or pets. Or call the local hospital, and say you have a few weeks free in which you could be a volunteer.

Right now you have to go beyond your sorrow. And write again, if you need to.

Can I Experience Heaven for Myself?

Several years ago, I visited Paris in a dream. The dream showed remarkable detail, right down to the wallpaper in the hotel room.

Heaven, like Paris, is seen differently by each person who goes there. My impressions about Paris before arrival would have been more flighty, had it not been for the dream that outlined what things to expect there.

Our concept of heaven is likewise a starry-eyed fantasy. Soul Travel is a personal way to see heaven here and now. Once we see it, then we arrange our lives to better advantage both now and in eternity.

We want heaven to be jeweled cities of light (and there are such), with angels flitting about like butterflies in a garden (there are those things too), but we yearn to tramp the hallowed heights in the company of saints, engaging them in sober debates that run into the ages. What a dull, empty, dreary, and dreadfully useless heaven!

Mercy and grace alone take no one to God Consciousness. That is a hoax perpetrated by religious thinkers, and it has misled countless laypeople in the mainstream religions.

Soul Travel is a spiritual journey that outpaces the Universal Mind kingdom. It delivers Soul to the Soul Plane, where we enter into the initial stage of self-knowledge.

Traveling the Spiritual Worlds

The Cheyenne Indians came from the area of the Great Lakes. First they lived in wigwams; and then gradually, as they were pushed westward by the white man, they began living in tepees. They did not have TV and radio, of course, and so they needed entertainment. They were people very much like us in many ways. They had their storytellers; and when a good storyteller traveled through, it was considered an event. He was invited in, given some food, and treated really well.

It was interesting the way the Indian storyteller would tie one story to another. After talking for a while he would say, "And this story leads to another." He'd talk awhile longer and then say, "This story ties in to another," and so on. Between stories they would sit around and have a good time—a commercial break.

Paul Twitchell, the founder of Eckankar, once said that writing a story is very easy: it's like stringing beads—one after another after another. The string goes from here to there. A storyteller would do that too. He would connect one story to another, which would tie in to another, and then there would be another one—like a rest point in eternity—and on and on.

The inner planes are this way, also. There is the Physical, and then there is the Astral. You take a little break, and then you go to the Causal; take a little break, Mental; then to the Etheric; on to the Soul Plane; and from there you go on into the spiritual God Worlds where you find the Sound and Light of ECK at that temple within yourself.

It is in these worlds that you take the journey to Self-Realization and God-Realization.

The God Worlds of ECK

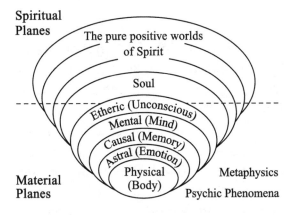

A Spiritual Exercise for Soul Travel

$\mathcal{I}$f you are interested in exploring the inner worlds through Soul Travel, you can try this technique tonight in the dream state.

HU (pronounced like the word *hue*) is an ancient love song to God. Before sleep, close your eyes and place your attention very gently on the Spiritual Eye (a point between and behind the eyebrows). Sing *HU*, and fill yourself with love.

This feeling of love is needed to give you the confidence to go forward into an unknown, unexplored area. One way to fill yourself with love is by calling up the warm memory of a past occasion that filled you with pure love.

Then look inwardly for the individual who is your ideal at this time—whether it is Christ or one of the ECK Masters. In a very gentle way, say, "I give you permission to take me to the place that I have earned for my greatest spiritual unfoldment." And then silently or out loud, continue to chant *HU*, *God*, or another holy word.

Try to visualize yourself walking into the inner worlds, and know that the individual who comes to meet you is a dear friend.

If it doesn't work the first time, do it again and again. The spiritual exercises are like physical exercises: before your muscles grow strong, you have to exercise them a number of times; it doesn't always happen in one try. It's quite likely that if you take up an exercise routine for thirty days, you're going to be stronger than you were at the beginning.

It's the same way with the spiritual exercises. The purpose of the Spiritual Exercises of ECK is simply to open a conduit, or a channel, between yourself and the Holy Spirit, which we know as the Audible Life Stream—the wave that comes from the heart of God. From the moment you begin singing *HU* and looking for truth in this particular way, whether you are conscious of it or not, changes are being made in you.

We come to know the reality of God as it is revealed through Divine Spirit, the Voice of God, which can be heard as Sound and seen as Light.

This is the secret path to heaven.

NEXT STEPS IN
SPIRITUAL EXPLORATION

- **Try a spiritual exercise.**
  Review the spiritual exercises in this book.
  Experiment with them.

- **Browse our Web site: www.Eckankar.org.**
  Watch videos; get free books, answers to
  FAQs, and more info.

- **Attend an Eckankar event** in your area.
  Visit "Eckankar around the World" on our
  Web site.

- **Read additional books** about the ECK
  teachings.

- **Explore advanced spiritual study** with the
  Eckankar discourses that come with annual
  membership.

- **Call or write to us:** Call 1-800-LOVE GOD
  (1-800-568-3463, toll-free, automated) or
  (952) 380-2200 (direct).

  Write to ECKANKAR, Dept. BK122, PO Box
  2000, Chanhassen, MN 55317-2000 USA.

FOR FURTHER READING
By Harold Klemp

ECK Wisdom on Conquering Fear

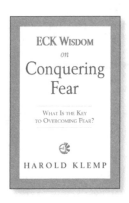

Would having more courage and confidence help you make the most of this lifetime?

Going far beyond typical self-help advice, this booklet invites you to explore divine love as the antidote to anxiety and the doorway to inner freedom.

You will discover ways to identify the karmic roots of fear and align with your highest ideals.

Use this book to soar beyond your limitations and reap the benefits of self-mastery.

Live life to its fullest potential!

Spiritual Wisdom on Health and Healing

This booklet is rich with spiritual keys to greater health on every level.

Discover the spiritual roots of illness and how gratitude can open your heart to God's love and healing.

Simple spiritual exercises go deep to help you get personal divine guidance and insights.

Revitalize your connection with the true healing power of God's love.

Spiritual Wisdom on Relationships

Find the answers to common questions of the heart including the truth about Soul mates, how to strengthen a marriage, and how to know if a partnership is worth developing.

The spiritual exercises included in this  booklet can help you break a pattern of poor relationships and find balance. You'll learn new ways to open your heart to love and enrich your relationship with God.

This booklet is a key for anyone wanting more love to give, more love to get, and better relationships with everyone in your life.

Spiritual Wisdom on Prayer, Meditation, and Contemplation

Bring balance and wonder to your life!

This booklet is a portal to your direct, personal connection with Divine Spirit.

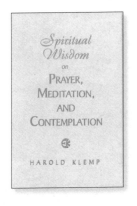

Harold Klemp shows how you can experience the powerful benefits of contemplation—"a conversation with the most secret, most genuine, and most mysterious part of yourself."

Move beyond traditional meditation via dynamic spiritual exercises. Learn about the uplifting chant of HU (an ancient holy name for God), visualization, creative imagination, and other active techniques.

Spiritual Wisdom on Karma and Reincarnation

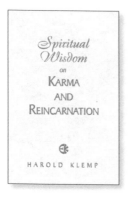

Have you lived before? What is the real meaning of life?

Discover your divine destiny—to move beyond the limits of karma and reincarnation and gain spiritual freedom.

This booklet reveals the purpose of living and the keys to spiritual growth.

You'll find answers to age-old questions about fate, destiny, and free will. These gems of wisdom can enhance your relationships, health, and happiness—and offer the chance to resolve all your karma in this lifetime!

Spiritual Wisdom on Dreams

This dream study will help you be more *awake* than you've ever been!

Spiritual Wisdom on Dreams reveals the most ancient of dream teachings for a richer and more productive life today.

In this dynamic booklet, author Harold Klemp shows you how to remember your dreams, apply dream wisdom to everyday situations, recognize prophetic dreams, and more.

You will be introduced to the art of dream interpretation and offered techniques to discover the treasures of your inner worlds.

ECK Wisdom on Inner Guidance

Looking for answers, guidance, protection?

Help can come as a nudge, a dream, a vision, or a quiet voice within you. This book offers new ways to connect with the ever-present guidance of ECK, the Holy Spirit. Start today!

Discover how to listen to the Voice of God; attune to your true self; work with an inner guide; benefit from dreams, waking dreams, and Golden-tongued Wisdom; and ignite your creativity to solve problems.

Each story, technique, and spiritual exercise is a doorway to greater confidence and love for life.

Open your heart and let God's voice speak to you!

The Call of Soul

Discover how to find spiritual freedom in this lifetime and the infinite world of God's love for you. Includes a CD with dream and Soul Travel techniques.

HU, the Most Beautiful Prayer

Singing *HU*, the ancient name for God, can open your heart and lead you to a new understanding of yourself. Includes a CD of the HU song.

Past Lives, Dreams, and Soul Travel

These stories and exercises help you find your true purpose, discover greater love than you've ever known, and learn that spiritual freedom is within reach.

The Spiritual Exercises of ECK

This book is a staircase with 131 steps leading to the doorway to spiritual freedom, self-mastery, wisdom, and love. A comprehensive volume of spiritual exercises for every need.

The Road to Spiritual Freedom, Mahanta Transcripts, Book 17

Every single moment of your life is the handiwork of a higher cause. And you can know what it is. Hint: God's love is the key, and spiritual freedom is the goal.

How to Survive Spiritually in Our Times, Mahanta Transcripts, Book 16

Discover how to reinvent yourself spiritually—to thrive in a changing world. Stories, tools, techniques, and spiritual insights to apply in your life now.

Autobiography of a Modern Prophet

This riveting story of Harold Klemp's climb up the Mountain of God will help you discover the keys to your own spiritual greatness.

Those Wonderful ECK Masters

Would you like to have *personal* experience with spiritual masters that people all over the world—since the beginning of time—have looked to for guidance, protection, and divine love? This book includes real-life stories and spiritual exercises to meet eleven ECK Masters.

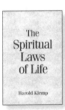

The Spiritual Laws of Life

Learn how to keep in tune with your true spiritual nature. Spiritual laws reveal the behind-the-scenes forces at work in your daily life.

Available at bookstores, online booksellers, or directly from Eckankar: www.ECKBooks.org; (952) 380-2200; ECKANKAR, Dept. BK122, PO Box 2000, Chanhassen, MN 55317-2000 USA.

GLOSSARY

Words set in SMALL CAPS are defined elsewhere in this glossary.

Blue Light   How the MAHANTA often appears in the inner worlds to the CHELA or seeker.

chela   A spiritual student. Often refers to a member of ECKANKAR.

ECK   The Life Force, the Holy Spirit, or Audible Life Current which sustains all life.

Eckankar *EHK-ahn-kahr*   Religion of the Light and Sound of God. Also known as the Ancient Science of SOUL TRAVEL. A truly spiritual religion for the individual in modern times. The teachings provide a framework for anyone to explore their own spiritual experiences. Established by PAUL TWITCHELL, the modern-day founder, in 1965. The word means Co-worker with God.

ECK Masters   Spiritual Masters who can assist and protect people in their spiritual studies and travels. The ECK Masters are from a long line of God-Realized Souls who know the responsibility that goes with spiritual freedom.

Fubbi Quantz *FOO-bee KWAHNTS* The guardian of the Shariyat-Ki-Sugmad at the Katsupari Monastery in northern Tibet. He was the Mahanta, the Living ECK Master during the time of Buddha, about 500 BC.

God-Realization The state of God Consciousness. Complete and conscious awareness of God.

Gopal Das *GOH-pahl DAHS* The guardian of the Shariyat-Ki-Sugmad at the Temple of Askleposis on the Astral Plane. He was the Mahanta, the Living ECK Master in Egypt, about 3000 BC.

HU *HYOO* The most ancient, secret name for God. It can be sung as a love song to God aloud or silently to oneself to align with God's love.

initiation Earned by a member of Eckankar through spiritual unfoldment and service to God. The initiation is a private ceremony in which the individual is linked to the Sound and Light of God.

Karma, Law of The Law of Cause and Effect, action and reaction, justice, retribution, and reward, which applies to the lower or psychic worlds: the Physical, Astral, Causal, Mental, and Etheric Planes.

Klemp, Harold The present MAHANTA, the LIVING ECK MASTER. SRI Harold Klemp became the Mahanta, the Living ECK Master in 1981. His spiritual name is WAH Z.

Living ECK Master The spiritual leader of ECKANKAR. He leads SOUL back to God. He teaches in the physical world as the Outer Master and in the spiritual worlds as the Inner Master. SRI HAROLD KLEMP became the MAHANTA, the Living ECK Master in 1981.

Mahanta An expression of the ECK, the Spirit of God that is always with you. The highest state of consciousness known on earth, only embodied in the LIVING ECK MASTER.

planes The levels of existence, such as the Physical, Astral, Causal, Mental, Etheric, and SOUL Planes.

Self-Realization SOUL recognition. The entering of Soul into the Soul PLANE and there beholding Itself as pure Spirit. A state of seeing, knowing, and being.

Shariyat-Ki-Sugmad *SHAH-ree-aht-kee-SOOG-mahd* The sacred scriptures of ECKANKAR. The scriptures are comprised of twelve volumes in the spiritual worlds. The first two were transcribed from the inner PLANES by PAUL TWITCHELL, modern-day founder of Eckankar.

Soul The True Self, an individual, eternal spark of God. The inner, most sacred part of each person. Soul is the creative center of Its own world.

Soul Travel   The expansion of consciousness. The ability of Soul to transcend the physical body and travel into the spiritual worlds of God. Soul Travel is taught only by the Living ECK Master. It helps people unfold spiritually and can provide proof of the existence of God and life after death.

Sound and Light of ECK   The Holy Spirit. The two aspects through which God appears in the lower worlds. People can experience them by looking and listening within themselves and through Soul Travel.

Spiritual Exercises of ECK   Daily practices for direct, personal experience with the Sound Current. Creative techniques using contemplation and the singing of sacred words to bring the higher awareness of Soul into daily life.

Sri *SREE*   A title of spiritual respect, similar to reverend or pastor, used for those who have attained the Kingdom of God. In Eckankar, it is reserved for the Mahanta, the Living ECK Master.

Sugmad *SOOG-mahd*   A sacred name for God. It is the source of all life, neither male nor female, the Ocean of Love and Mercy.

Temples of Golden Wisdom These Golden Wisdom Temples are spiritual temples which exist on the various PLANES—from the Physical to the Anami Lok; CHELAS of ECKANKAR are taken to the temples in the SOUL body to be educated in the divine knowledge; the different sections of the SHARIYAT-KI-SUGMAD, the sacred teachings of ECK, are kept at these temples.

Twitchell, Paul An American ECK MASTER who brought the modern teachings of ECKANKAR to the world through his writings and lectures. His spiritual name is Peddar Zaskq.

Wah Z The spiritual name of SRI HAROLD KLEMP. It means the secret doctrine. It is his name in the spiritual worlds.

For more explanations of ECKANKAR terms, see *A Cosmic Sea of Words: The ECKANKAR Lexicon* by Harold Klemp.

80

About the Author

Author Harold Klemp is known as a pioneer of today's focus on "everyday spirituality." He was raised on a Wisconsin farm and attended divinity school. He also served in the US Air Force.

In 1981, after years of training, he became the spiritual leader of Eckankar, Religion of the Light and Sound of God. His full title is Sri Harold Klemp, the Mahanta, the Living ECK Master. His mission is to help people find their way back to God in this life.

Each year, Harold Klemp speaks to thousands of seekers at Eckankar seminars. Author of more than one hundred books, he continues to write, including many articles and spiritual-study discourses. His inspiring and practical approach to spirituality helps many thousands of people worldwide find greater freedom, wisdom, and love in their lives.